The Fish-Wife

PACIFIC POETRY SERIES

The Fish-Wife

poems by
Cynthia Huntington

University of
Hawaii Press
Honolulu

The Fish-Wife was selected by
David Wagoner in the
1985 Pacific Poetry Series
Competition

Library of Congress Catalog Card No. 85-52065
ISBN 0-8248-1051-1

For Bert and Sam

Contents

I

The Desire to Shine Without Burning　3
Migraine　4
What the Weatherman Said　6
The Fish-Wife　8
The Length of the Hour　10
February　11
Day Labor　13
Burn　17

II

The Lake　21
In Our Former Life　22
Vermont　26
The Mountain　27
Night Watch—The Westland Mines　29
Patchwork　31
Material Evidence　37
There　38

III

No One　43
Cast Iron District at Dawn　45
The Holiday Suicides　46
The Year of the Horse　48
Heat Lightning　51
Patrick　53
The Fault　55
Lagos: Target Practice　57
Recovery　59
Talking to Myself　61
Fire　62

IV

Not the Atlantic　65
Herring Cove　66
We Have Lived in Great Houses　67
The Rock　70
The Season　71
Wings　72
From Exile　73

Acknowledgements

Some of the poems in this book have appeared in: *The Agni Review, The Country Journal, Crazy Horse, Green House, Harvard Magazine, The Montana Review, Nimrod, Ploughshares, Shankpainter,* and *The Virginia Quarterly Review.*

Grateful acknowledgement is made to the Corporation of Yaddo, The Massachusetts Artists Foundation, and the National Endowment for the Arts for generous support during the writing of this book.

Special thanks to the Fine Arts Work Center in Provincetown for support, fellowship and community through many winters. I am endebted to Donald Hall, Cleopatra Mathis and Norman Williams for their comments on the manuscript in progress.

I

THE DESIRE TO SHINE WITHOUT BURNING

The full moon is high above the city tonight.
It has paused between the towers of the World Trade Center,
perfectly balanced, and indifferent. The cat is asleep
on the green rug, belly-up, while trucks below
gnash their gears at the light,
breathe hard, and accelerate toward the river.

Nothing else seems to want love
or to stare at the moon with desire. The river unwinds
its length alongside the city, shining
with a mineral brilliance, when stars float
among the spilled bodies of oil. There are nights
when the sky is opaque and final, no face,
and the black water does not move at all.

Moon, blind eye opening and closing,
I am here, down here where the cat is asleep
and trucks, growling out of reach,
rattle the joints of the bridges in rage.
Couples hesitate between streetlamps
and go on. I can hear
their voices fall away like water,
water falling over rocks,
and I am the only one talking to the moon.

I would like to be silent, move as I was made
into darkness and back, never bargain
for love or change before it. All things
which are serene receive light, which is a grace
given, a grace also unfolding
to receive. Fix me, let me know
how to move and stand still, to be bright
then invisible without dying. Give me
blessing like water continually flowing
—a light not my own, not the river's.

MIGRAINE

"Today it is suddenly winter," a voice
outside me is saying. From the cheerless
stairwell I enter the street—cold sunlight
on fenders, sidewalks white with it.
The pain that started behind my left eye
moved like a hand down my neck, across
shoulders, the top vertebrae of the spine,
working down, rooting in. As I cross the street
my feet hit the pavement in a series of small shocks
—the bones of the feet, legs,
tight spaces between the knobs of the backbone,
all take it. Walking is a rhythm
like the blood forced up to the brain,
banging of metal doors in the wind at night.
I knew when I woke up
and saw the furniture in my rooms
ready to move out on its own, the rugs uneasy
over linoleum, and every chair awkward
and arbitrary in its position, I knew
I'd have trouble convincing myself
things are going all right. Lies
I keep telling myself are breeding like viruses.
I knew when you left this morning
I couldn't sleep it off. Pain takes me
to the center or spins me in circles
trying to get away. *Don't say "spin."*
It's working deeper now; something is dead
in my stomach, something I need to get rid of.
The truth of my life is so big I can't not see it.
It is alive in my bedsheets, in the whine
of the refrigerator; it is in these shoes,
the skins of dead animals nobody mourned. Dead things
can't ask for help. For many, that is the first sign.
I asked for this, my hand shaking
when I pay the woman in the drugstore; I must have asked
for this, it must be my fault; this life has rules
and something of my own is claiming me. I'll take
my own pain back again. Now, outcast,
it keeps attacking me in restaurants, in grocery stores,

at home, and on the street. Sometimes it won't let go,
as today, binding my legs and arms and demanding
confessions. I confess to crimes
against all the people of pain.
I am bringing the exiles home. That banging
of metal doors against brick I listened to all night
was just some more pain wanting in. Come in:
live in the center, hated, take everything.
Let's get it over; what does this world ever give
that it doesn't take back again? We can keep our pain;
we can keep dying. When the body dies it grows stiff
and swells with all it had kept to itself. Finally
the skin bursts and it all rushes out, stinking, and then
the body lets everything in. Grass, earth, other bodies.
We can't come to that yet.
We have to keep walking around in our bodies.
We have to keep finding arms to lie down in.
We have to get up and feed ourselves on the dead things.
We have to keep walking around with our pain
right inside us, or all the pain in the world will rush
through like an army, raping and burning,
tearing up everything because it can't find
where it belongs—its home, in us, where it began.

WHAT THE WEATHERMAN SAID

"This is not the beginning of the Ice Age.
This is January." Though tonight heavy snows
bury Colorado and children are lost
on the Plains where a school bus drifts empty
on an empty road and small figures wander miles
past help, the storm will find us
in Massachusetts, forewarned and unafraid.

Ice quiets the rumbling Mississippi, and Illinois
goes dark a hundred miles across.
In the North Atlantic sea ice increases
each year, while prevailing winds change, wild
on the land, snapping power lines and shattering
barns into rubble of lumber. Still, we know
the extreme is not always abnormal.

Meanwhile the couple upstairs
are discussing their future in screams
above the sound of gunfire in Detroit
and she recommends he remove himself directly
to hell. I hear a fist slam wood,
the girl's sharp cry, and I think
they are not even real. They are abnormal.

What is real is the film they show later
of the shy rhinoceros shot down
by tranquilizer darts; crumbling into his skin, huge
knees breaking, he goes down and they drag him
into the truck and take him to a sanctuary
for the endangered, the nearly extinct,
where he eats so delicately whole branches of pine.

It is a fact the world has gotten too dangerous
for animals. But not for us!
And though tonight the thousand disasters
are broadcast, and families stand stunned
beside burned houses—their stored-up lives
they thought belonged in a box—
though tomorrow's murderer is waiting to confess

and will not be believed, we will sleep
assured of reports, warnings from the world we know.
The Great Lakes are frozen hard now
and across the Adirondacks a light snow
begins covering the fir and spruce, white on the edges,
dark beneath. In a small poor country my sleep
is being made safe by men with guns.

Tonight someone is being beaten to make me safe;
some small poor person has a dangerous idea; he wants
another life. He will not appear tonight;
he is nearly extinct; he is going away.
Now the storm is with him, walking
before him, and now the various animals who die
and are buried in ice, consumed

in the time of continents, before roads begin
or names of cities. The land changes now; just so
we will change without knowing
into another creature. And though the snow in Colorado
is immeasurable, filling each valley, moving east
toward us, this is not the beginning
as it is not the end. This is January, Massachusetts.
There is still time.

THE FISH-WIFE

I'll take a bath when it snows,
when I can look out the window up high
and see the sky all pale
and blank like a fish's eye.
And I know the boats won't go out tonight,
the fishermen drinking whiskey, locked
in a bar-dream, the music rocking them deeper.

It doesn't snow enough here,
though some would say otherwise,
fearing accidents. But the paper boy, skidding
uphill on his bike in light snow, knows better,
making S-tracks when his wheels slide sideways.

We really needed this snow, the old men will say,
putting to bed the surface roots of trees,
putting to bed the too-travelled streets.

When everything is covered
the earth has a light of its own;
the snow falls down from the moon
as everyone knows, and brings that light
back to us. I needed this light.

All day I kept by the window, watching the sky,
a prisoner in my clothes, the wind felt dry
and mean. Starlings stalked the yard with evil eyes
—I hated them, and hated, too, my neighbor's house
where sparks from the chimney fell back in a stinking
cloud—black ashes bringing no blessing.

When the roads are covered,
when the water is black and snow falls
into the waves, the birds' hunger swirls
the air, dark lovely shapes. All hungers
are equal now. I'll give them bread and seeds.

I have no money; the whiskey is gone,
and I must bathe in water. Fishermen, please
do not go out in your flimsy boats tonight
to chase after the cod and mackerel,
to hook the giant eels. Go safe,
go free. Let your feet leave trails
through streets and yards, wandering
home, your crooked voyages to bed.

THE LENGTH OF THE HOUR

New houses relax on the fields.
Garage doors open soundlessly
to admit the monster. Tires stretched
over forty pounds of air
pressure float across gravel.

The boy closes the last storm
door on the last evening
paper and runs to the car
where his mother waits. She does not
answer him; the door slam freezes
her dreams. It is January.

A dog chained to a barn door
keeps barking. Somebody's angry,
scared to let him go.
On the other side
of a forest past these fields,
wolves sniff the hard snow
of the tundra. I lay beside the only
tree for warmth, there
where the pack might find me.

The house takes care of us now.
Look at the meat
browning under the light.
The refrigerator switches on;
ice crashes into the tray.

Here are locks in case someone
wants to do us harm. Remember
how the police had to pound and pound
to wake us that night a white Cadillac
leapt from the icy road

into the arms of our maple! It hung there,
empty, doors flung wide—
it was a great white petal of a car,
breathing under the gas-lights, opening
and opening.

FEBRUARY

It's raining and I think of you.
The wet mounds of pitted snow
sag against fences, the brown yards,
wavering antennas, and tree limbs
full of electric wires, the weeds
charged with rain stuttering
in patches between curb and driveway. Sky
with no light, these greasy black
telephone poles unmoving, planted
like stakes in the earth,
holding up unearthly cables, and grasping
the looped wires, small ones and heavy ones,
that meet in the transformers'
translating engines, and speak.
The stillness, the power,
the blank houses when no one is home
and the dark inside is greater,
deeper than this no-color sky—
intrigue of a single car passing,
its loud, even rumble, the brief glimpse
of a man's head and shoulders,
and after-image of rain
thrown up by the wheels in cool sparks.

It's raining and I do not think of you.
I am thinking instead of my whole life,
how what is missing cries out in it
and gathers each odd detail
to the exact shape of what is so
strongly lacked, it may seem to appear
in the space that is left.
How each grass blade, distinct, rises
out of wet earth, leaning,
bent and played by air, and the bright
yellow stripe of the curb crumbles
along the ridges. Looped wires
hang silent; branches surround them
without touching. The low places
in pavement start to fill with brown water
flowing over, thin streams joining

widening pools, black as asphalt,
and circles bursting where each drop
is welcomed. When rain is the only
light thrown down, brown water
overflows itself in streams, and in each dark,
dark pool, light from the lightless
sky shines up.

DAY LABOR

In noon sun the white enamel is twice bright,
thick shining in the pail.
My arm aches, reaching up for hours,
the ladder rungs pressing my shins in grooves
—wood on bone. I bend to dip the brush again,
lapping it over, painting white on white—

a white so clear it has all colors in it,
pure, warm as midday, all hot light melting.
Blue water rises and falls under the boards,
all day the blue lights shining up
beneath this wharf where the summer cottages
crouch, swayed back and forth by tides.

Here on the North Atlantic
wind strips color, salt eats wood,
and the world turns grey and silver all winter.
Finally the gun-metal sheen of the ocean.
In spring I am up on a ladder all day,
the other element of change—repair.
I scrape, paint over, the old boards shine
wet, and sweat beads my neck, sweet

these first hot days, no shade, the sun so high.
At night my body hurts, imparticularly all over,
and my dreams are stunned and simple,
repeating the brush strokes, lapping
cracked, worn boards, the glare
bleaching everything white—repeating

the Portuguese talk of the women,
night language to my ears, sung and shouted
over the pails' clamor and doors
barking in wind. My dreams
play everything back. Was there something
I missed, a last detail the mind insists on
holding, out of the days' unvarying rhythm?
No word, the sky is beautiful, water

makes slow brushing noises against the pilings,
in and out, the black shadow of my arm on the wall.
The days pass slowly like this, so calm.
The summer people will see it. They sit
and watch shadows move over the boards.
Like this. They say it is so lovely

they might die here content.
They say this far from their lives,
imagining death like a foreign waiter:
quietly he offers something covered on a tray,
leans in close, whispers.
You can pretend you do not understand.

The paint smells like flowers. A bee
is dying in it, dragging a white foot
behind, struggling to fly
with that suffocating nectar.
A hammer beats overhead like a single idea.
Down the street a drill hacks into concrete,
jolting someone's bones, and it is endless,
this restoration of the world I do not own.

I could be anything under this sky,
but here I am no one. I am my hands, my body's
strength and patience, one of the ones
who were here, who built and repaired
and built over. There is no place for my name.
And if I once believed

that the one thing, carefully attended,
might bring to pass another world,
like this one, but transformed by some
intrinsic, so far unnoticed light—no more.
If I thought by doing the one thing over
and over, with attention,
I might make it all visible, that life
which is here unseen, just waiting

to occur—no, I do not think
the world can have a truer self than this.
Then what is it for, this light
on blue water like silver rising,
this light in the mind responding?

At 2 we have coffee. At 4 we go home.
Nothing stays in my mind now, just forward,
urging the day ahead, the clock's hands
opening and closing. I hardly need

the clock now, learning at what angle
the sun crosses, a shadow eclipsing
the lip of the pail. There is a rougher measure
in the tide's reach, when it goes out
and the pigeons return to roost under the planks.
Then the water rises
and they fly off again. Brown sand

dries to gold, then darkens from beneath.
I could count the day in brush strokes,
advance and return, the slow, repeating
progress over boards. I will know
when I get there, when it is time.

I stand out to sea on my ladder sailing
the current, and I am no one.
And it does not end.
And I might believe, but there is nothing
to believe unless that other life
will show itself right now,

where I am, where I have stayed and waited,
will place me here truly
for the first time. These slow hours,

quiet days spent nearly alone
in company of gulls and distant voices.
Soon the summer people will come back,
and then they will go away
and then return. It is noon by the sun,
May, and I've done nothing
winter into spring, to say I was here.
To say where I am going—

Light on blue water like silver rising.

I am losing my time.
After work I walk home
in my old clothes, cuffs flapping,
paint on my hands
like spots of noon light shining back.
Night, sometimes foghorns
saying over and over, they remain
in their place. All night I'll be painting

propped on a high ladder, not letting go my hold,
my balance, here on top of the swaying world.

BURN

I step outside, my arms clutching
the brown bags tight, and I'm lost,
caught up in the wind's hollow, pulling away
from the house, the house left standing
stark in a circle of brown grass. Clouds,
whipped cirrus, freeze in the high layers.
Late November, taste of what is.

This morning I pulled back the curtain
and saw how old everything is. Cars
bumped their axles on the railroad tracks
and the trellis sagged under bare vines.
Old glass, old wood, the window chattered
under my hand. In the bare yard the house
stands suspicious, stiff-sided, uncertain
of its right to be here. Who is certain?
At night the wind speaks with my father's
voice—angry I still live alone—
and the trains wrap their high, wild notes
against the hill, flinging themselves
away from this time, this place.

Two days' news, potato peels, coffee, eggshells,
cigarette ashes black and damp.
I bury the food scraps in compost;
they'll make their own heat, live
on that slow death all winter. Now light
the papers stuffed in the grate, poke them
so everything burns. Rows of corn stubble
point south and a storm-stunted tree leans
sharply away, like someone bent over coughing.

I stand erect, a too-thin woman in a brown coat
that flaps at my legs, wrapping me tight
then unpeeling to fly up like a sail.
My head insect-small in a cap, my feet
stuck into a man's boots that hold me
down as the sparks fly upward, hot and red,

and then the sooty pieces falling back.
—Ashes that sift and blow away
like evil snow, a message to another county.

Careful!—a page of yesterday's news lifts up,
a paper lantern blown full and rising
toward tree limbs, pulsing.
Fire in the branches; a squirrel's nest is shot
with light, and it is the sun falling red
behind it, right there where the world drops off.
I stare into smoke, down the tracks past ruined
garden rows, turning the poker over, stirring
dirt and ashes till my hands go black. Hold

nothing. A new trembling in my legs rises
out of the moving ground. In the quick fall
of darkness a single red eye hurtles out of the west
—something the sun shot back. The train
pounds the earth, shaking up roots and seeds,
shaking the house set deep in the ground, bed-
rock, bones of my fathers. It shakes me
where I stand, in this place that is my body,
drawn up from this black earth and falling
back. And after me no more. And it cries
for me, what I could not say, with one cry for its
coming and going—a single, sustained high note
that only the distance bends.

II

THE LAKE

You wade into the water
as if you were stepping off the world.
You go far out,
where I can't follow, where water
is one color with the sky, and you
between them, emerging, going under.

Water does not exist; the night
has taken your legs. You are in the sky
with night above and below you.
Your half-body stands, turns;
you dip the bucket into the sky

and carry it back to me, brimming
with night, and you pour into my arms
the heavy night. You fill my arms
with water; I feel it cold against me
and you turn and go back to fill the bucket again.

In your high boots, your father's boots,
you can wade into the water
and nothing can touch you. You only lose
half your body. Come back
and help me carry this basin
of darkness uphill without spilling.
When we wash ourselves in this water
we will be invisible all night.

IN OUR FORMER LIFE

1

We lived 40 bends
down the road past town
in a house the minister's family left,
chilled and bare.
In the barn, nothing
but rotting stalls, turds white as ash,
and the loneliest old dog nobody
ever wanted, left behind to howl
and stink, and wear out her teeth on the wires.

I was a girl, sweeping
the steps with a gesture.
I cut the heads of the peonies
to float in bowls. Ants hesitated
on the lips of drowned petals,
touching antennas, in conference:
there must be a way out.

You shot birds in the woods
and carried them home by their feet
and split them open and pulled out their bones.
You picked their skulls and eyesockets clean,
stretched skins over carved forms,
posed all over the house. Glass eyes,
wire tensing the claws, the almost invisible
stitches where the knife entered.

You were still a boy who killed things
and sat down to put them back together.
The day you shot the mother hawk
and carried the babies home in your coat
I heard you behind the door, offering food
in a coaxing voice; how badly you wanted
them to live with us! One lived

to bite your hand in rage, tearing
the flesh between thumb and forefinger, that bled
in dark circles across the floor
as you carried the hand, immobile, to water.

Later I cried to watch you unwrap
the dressings to show me how fierce
his beak was. You seemed proud
and angry at once. You said you'd get a leash
for that bird, a harness, and you'd train it
to fly from your arm like a falcon.

That night in bed
your left hand touched me, clumsy with gauze,
and I thought of two wounds meeting,
how a hand will close
on its secret, vulnerable part.

2

Each night I lay among your creatures—
small birds in flight, others with claws flexed
for the kill. The little bat hung upside down,
staring at us without accusation
as we listened to the forgotten hound
howl in the barn, our insane relative.

Soon, before sleep took us,
we would get up and dress in the dark
in the room without lamps, and leave
the bed with one blanket folded back,
and leave the empty house shining
with its creature eyes, and go out
to ease the car without lights
down the rutted drive. The bright rooms
of our parents' houses waited up
full of argument. I remember

how in that bare room
by the bare window we would touch
the whole lengths of our bodies
all along, pressing
thigh and belly, chest and arms—
bodies still new to touch, tender
and violent, owning that first world
where weeds sang back to the garden, gone
three times to seed: the house was ours.

In the rough grain of those floor-boards
my blood soaked, deeper than nails,
that first afternoon in yellow light
when I cried and pulled from you and ran
ashamed and wounded, leaving dark circles
in the wood—stains you'd tell your father
were from some large bird you killed
and carried in too soon.

I was less a girl each day,
cleaning the fish we caught in the pond,
small as my hand, and full of bones.

I was less a girl, though nothing wild.
To live again, I would learn patience
—what to hold, what holds me. I have still
a white triangle on my thigh, scar
of a miscast hook you removed that summer
with a pocket knife, slicing
clean, proud you knew just
what to do. We washed the blood
with pond water, and fish swam around my legs
—the colors of light, shapes of water,
a live current, cold to the touch.

VERMONT

Woodsmoke in July—though the nights
were not bitter, we were cold in ourselves
and wanted the branches to light.
Each room had its fire, alone, and the breath
of woodsmoke followed me, walking,
and though I kept my head down, walking,
I was with them, I was always there.

Everyone seemed sad for no reason
and the words overheard as I passed
were reassuring, mountain speech
against the stars that missed us, falling
every time. That they had to fall,
that we were not included.

It happened that the night was too thin;
I could hear everyone talking and I'd wish I was drunk,
but I wouldn't be. Thinking now I could get
drunk on woodsmoke, thinking odors have no names
so we can't call them, but they call us, burning
and we can't answer, can't say mountain I remember
but I don't need to come back, not ever, not yet.

THE MOUNTAIN

Grass is a green fire, hissing in rain.
Bushes press close to the path,
their breath of leaves on my neck—how hot
the world must be inside!

Now headlights climb the hill in pairs;
their beams divide the woods and pass on,
touching nothing here. Below,
windows are going out—one,
then one—then night dives in without breathing.

When stars
slide down the sky in August,
that is the last of them. How they streak
the moment, flung stones, falling
bodies! I want to touch myself
in the places where stars fell down,
my secret body pierced with light.

Tonight I know more are falling unseen,
passing close. Touching
the air, breath of this world, burns them,
extinguished beyond sight.

I want to touch myself with fire,
light the ways nerves reach to the skin,
branching, bending back, desires that won't
be contained. I wish I could lose
my mind for just a while, released to hear
just once those voices
in trees and rocks, anything speaking

—soul, hand, or voice—across the green
green tangled hills, over the rattle
of my heart, my feet thudding the ground,
to feel the whole mountain
alive around me, speechless.

I'm ashamed to be so lonely
as if some spirit were missing from the world
where nothing can be missing, where everything
that we are must be. Listen:

rain hits the leaves, counting—*first,*
first, first, unrepeating, touch only
perhaps felt. The trampled grass
breathes quietly back. No one there.

NIGHT WATCH—THE WESTLAND MINES

for Samuel Hulings (1907–1974)

At night there is no difference.
Headlights click off
and already you're going under.

The lamp on your forehead,
the skull's bone-white,
moves when you turn,
an eye scanning someone else's dream.

This is the world the insomniac knows
well, light batting the palpable
darkness, measuring day-carved rooms
with a single beam, all night walking
through the stone corridors.

Overhead your wife and children sleep.
There is nothing you can do for them now,
but you go on
down, see the understructure holds,
make certain no water is rising.

If the lamplight flickers, fading yellow,
then green, it may mean the long
sick vapor has been freed
from the rock. If the gas
crawls forward, swelling, you'll get out

fast, climb up where windows tilt
into that other night, let the bell
say it for you, what you have been thinking
all night: *wake up, wake up!*

If the lamp holds
steady, if the alarm is only
in your mind, go deeper.

The sleepless hold black hands
to black faces; disappearing
from themselves, they stumble
in and out of the earth. At night

there is no difference.
Now the old forests are black
dust in your skin and hair,
the whorls of your fingers
like fossil prints repeating. Go on;

far above the world begins
another day in smoke
lifted over houses, doors opening
to first light showing fields, fences,
roads down which cars are turning.

PATCHWORK

1. Cuttings

The odd pieces
collected slowly over years,
pieces too small
or rich for the usual patterns:
silks and taffetas, red
from a petticoat,
green soft drapery velvet.

Women cut and sewed, and saved
what fell from their cutting.

And everything that family wore,
whatever warmed them,
anything soft under their heads,
was made by women's hands.
Constant, the daily offering
held between their hands.

Out of the usual pattern of days,
this quilt with no pattern,
bright and odd, made
from richer days they saved for
and saved after, cutting.

2. Patterns

In Michigan evening a woman
looked out from her kitchen over dishes
and stared at the house next door
where only one window showed light.

In her house, growing sons moved
restless from room to room
as if the house were suddenly too small,
and she felt it
like the weeks before each birth
when they turned inside her,
wanting more than she could give.

Seven dark windows
and one with light; she looked
at the house where one woman lived alone
and all she said was, "Someday
one of us will be left here, too,"
and her husband said nothing.

3. Parts

When she was older, and stairs,
even door sills seemed perilous,
she moved everything into one room,
slept on the couch by the stove
and at night burned only one lamp
in the one room at the center of the house.

And the drawers and the closets and boxes
were not opened, rooms full of aging
treasures kept safe for no one, the cedar
trunks locked and feather mattresses
made up with sheets, pillowcases, quilts.

So many years passed; she forgot;
she continued her slow pulling away
from everything she might have remembered.

Then she left the house too.
With the table set for supper,
silverware and pills beside her plate,
she walked out the last time
and gave the keys to a stranger
in a real estate office. All she wanted
was a room, and she could find that anywhere.

4. Pieces

The widow next door phoned her son
who bought the house with everything in it
and sold the pieces at auction for twice
the price. For days they sorted and tagged,
and opened boxes filled with letters
written to people long dead, strangers

whose clothes hung in the wardrobes,
whose dishes were on the shelves; everything
had a price. Brass beds and antique dressers,
mahogany tables, and thick, velvet-bound albums.

He sold the uniforms saved from three wars,
the cast-iron pots, china door knobs, ivory
boxes for pins and hair combings, mirrors
with carved frames, carpets, and the three
cartons of Edison light bulbs, never opened.

He kept a silver brush and comb for his wife
and a quilt for each of his children.
In the nursing home, the old woman died
three weeks later. She had taken off her rings
the last night, and put them on the table beside her.

5. Stitches

The patchwork quilt was a wedding gift
offered like an heirloom by his parents
who could not tell who made it, or when.

Thinking it too old and fine to use,
we hung it on the wall. Often we would admire
the stitches which exaggerated the joining of pieces—
heavy embroidery thread shining yellow and blue,
criss-crossed, or like flowers bordering a walk.
We admired the patience in those stitches,
taken carefully, that held together
many lives in one story, a life out of the life,
using whatever was given.

We guessed what the pieces were—
this one a Sunday dress, that a brocade robe,
a baby's christening satin here, and the streaked
silk a ball gown, still giving off light.
We hung it on a wall for the colors, the incoherent
story of special occasions, in that room
where our own story broke, pulled apart in anger.

Too old to be of use
to us, that patience; there was strain,
then violence as china cups
rattled our rebellion and bookcases quivered
top-heavy in the corners. Promises
came down on our heads, ties gave,
and all our best work could not hold it together.

6. Joinings

One night, sleeping alone, I was cold
and I opened my eyes. On the far wall
the colors of the quilt vibrated
through the dark. I wanted it then.
I wanted to be part of its story,
comfort of years before that hard year,
warmth of lives discontinuous with mine,
the odd pieces joined beneath the surface
with tight, invisible stitches.

I thought of the spare bodies of women,
women who made quilts, who slept under them
and died, and I pulled it down
and wrapped it tight around me,
the weight of it pressing me, and I slept.
And sleeping, my breath passed over
the quilt, and the warmth of my body
that had been escaping, rose
and held in the layers of quilt.
And every breath in that pattern,
and every body that slept there, stirred
and slept with me.

What the breaths said was this:
that life outlasts the living,
the goods their makers, while the days
of the making are lost. In each life
what is left over still waits to be used.

But in the life lived strongly, nothing
is left over, there is nothing to look for.
When we find nothing ready-made, when nothing
whole is given, our offering is to join
the impossible, odd pieces, thread by thread
each day for what will serve. Our gift
will be knowing what to leave behind.

MATERIAL EVIDENCE

That winter there were no words for it at all.
Now nothing is left but objects,
the lies they tell in breaking. Insomnia
chipped sleep at the edges, until our dreams
grew sharp as glass. I marked off days
on the calendar, numbers that grew toward an ending
each time, starting over when I turned the page.

In April the ground started giving up bodies,
the half-digested snakes and rodents,
translucent wings of the largest insects.
Snow ran downhill in streams, filling the lake,
which started to move with that current,
carrying broken ice toward shore.
I remember the doe, chased down by dogs

in December, who leaped from the bank in terror,
crashed through ice, went down and froze there.
The thaw brought her finally across
and bumped her against the bank, but she couldn't
climb out, gripped by that cold that stops time,
though the sun was warming her, softening flesh.
And though we walked there without anger

there was space for another to stand between us.
It was a slow crossing; it was a winter without words,
and the cold stayed deep in the ground until May.
They fished her out with hooks; the body came apart,
disjointing as they lifted, and they laid her down
in a wooded place, away from the beach, this time
taken under, finished, this time no more.

THERE

These woods have no memory and do not end,
indistinct beyond the black tendons of pines
that twist upward into the air, holding themselves still.
Beyond, all blank and quiet now
snow falls straight down, no wind, almost
nothing moving, and I stand here nowhere staring
into the white space of everything that happens.
Grass and weeds stick through the pond's ice
like stubble in an open field, where once in Michigan
I stood at dusk. Black birds flew past me,
rising and falling, toward the far trees—
flew past me like a stone, or a shadow on the ground.
They seemed like something torn out of the earth,
its naked furrows broken at my feet. Behind me, windows
opened bright eyes at evening. I would not go back.

It's nearly dark now; snow surrounds me, forms
repeat and don't repeat, touching everything at once.
I want to stay here, like staying inside a memory
of a bad time, that is no longer painful. Now I see
how beautiful the trees always were,
the deep, responsive peace among them,
and tangled lines of cat-brier knotting
the world together, the muscular beauty of hills
and deep tracks some dog made running sideways along the ridge.

A jay, dull in snow-light, rattling branches overhead,
seems to call back every living thing I looked at
once, through a narrow window of sorrow
in a winter before he lived, when another
season's birds threw themselves hungrily into the sky.
It was not sorrow, but rage that slid over me like ice,
then, sealing the world in perfect, silent cold.
I was still, and in me nothing moved,
yet the seasons carried me with them, turned me
back and forward again, so I moved inside the years.

This storm began over the Great Lakes and travelled east;
it was in Michigan three days ago and kept on
to this coast where every weather ends, where storms
are lost at sea. I am here; I am lost.
And if, far back in Michigan, another storm falls into evening,
may I stand in another life? I would not go back.
That jay, flying off after some new
desire of his own, has been flying away from me for years—
generous messenger among the downward-drifting bodies,
hurrying though none will be saved. *Don't stop*,
I am telling him. I am here; I will be there soon,
where you are going.

III

NO ONE

There is no one at home tonight; no one can stay home.
The streets and the bars and the theatres
are crowded with lovers and would-be lovers, and you
are with them until I find you, my legs hurrying
up each street past all the other desires.
Sex is in the air, in the water, in piano keys, taxis,
and in long throats arching to swallow the cool liquid.
By the river men meet and go to dance
and push their tongues into each other's mouths, and boats
scrape against the piers, a sound heavy with longing,
while the small waves slap-slap and try to come between.

A siren is screaming like a woman when I walk out to find you.
Teen-age boys crowd the restaurant window
where a television star is eating dinner. They call
and chant and push against the glass; they wait for hours,
rubbing arms and bodies, sniff the air like young dogs.
The bum on the corner caresses an alleycat with his left hand.
She arches her back and rubs her thigh across his face
as he urges her to drink from his bottle. Dead men in the river
washed upstream in the embrace of weeds, and swimmers
who go out too far and return with larger eyes and mouths
swollen with salt. Lovers, lovers, no one alone.

Fingers clutch in hair, dancers are rubbing
against one another; that is why there is so much laughter.
Lovers run to the park and undress at the feet of statues—
stone horses, a soldier on guard who stands unmoved
above them, still silent if it is not love, if the girl
begins screaming, if the man runs, if the knife shines in the grass.
Feet on the pavement hurrying—where are you, where
are you tonight—the wind asks and asks, and laughter
flies out of mouths that are opened. Bright fish squirm
in the arteries, trying to get back to the heart.
Upstream in us, they make the pulse wild, until they find

their way, until the deep touch reaches.
I push on in the crowd, against the current of bodies,
swallow their breaths downwind, urgent until I find you
and we're swept into it, together clinging, as the street
catches fire and sirens raise their voices, crying for love,
the whole city screaming for love, until even God
who murdered his wives to live alone unchallenged
howls tonight in his celibate heaven. Statues wait under lights,
stone carved and beaten to resemble the living, stone
that glows with impossible desire, moving with the earth,
while the full moon submits and is slowly eaten alive.

CAST IRON DISTRICT AT DAWN

Far down the street an engine curses and starts.
The sound startles pigeons, waking to pick
crumbs in the gutter, their undisturbed hour.
Sunday: no one is going to work.
All down the wide street no one is walking.
A torn poster blown against a loft window
draws the eye upward; note
the building's outmoded grace which survives neglect,
the high-arched windows and generous double doors.
The warehouses closed today, the rooms
where women and children sewed, bent-backed from dawn
through evening, empty for years now and dark as ever.
Here—iron grilles locked against storefronts—
the newsstand's shuttered front denies responsibility
and the long street never turns to look back.
It is a sinister hour, after all. In doorways
men are waking who begrudge the couples upstairs
their morning sleep. Still, morning unaware
comes with its blue light into the city—
a bloodless sky whose light arrives modestly,
evenly in every corner with a true innocence
that does not discriminate. The air is cool,
smell of the sea nearby, the expectation of gulls.
Trees in the park shake their leafless branches
tenderly, and the sunken amphitheatre
around the fountain, and the stones arranged
in their lovely diagonals, invite you. This hour
belongs to no one. Its peacefulness disturbs you
because it is uncommitted, like the dream
in which only you survive the holocaust,
like your own future which you will make out of streets,
buildings, forgotten faces, faces not yet imagined.

THE HOLIDAY SUICIDES

It is the week before Thanksgiving.
From my office window I see the lights
come on at 4:00, up and down 2nd Avenue.
It has to do with the year ending,
this earlier darkness, these celebrations.
A line in the *News* says crisis centers
are training new volunteers
for the Christmas season. Everything
is ready for them. The weapons
are in drugstores and kitchen drawers.
Most of the things you own can be weapons;
even your own car will take you there
if you close the doors and keep driving
in the same place. The hospital attendants
with their beautiful white hands are on duty
and there are places in the ground
where no one is buried yet, that will take you in.
Lights go up in store windows; on the street
you pass people who don't know yet
they will decide to die. You
may be one of them—it may switch on in you
suddenly, what you are going to give yourself
this year. And there are always
the last-minute adventurers who put it off for weeks
and have to get drunk and smash their cars
in the last hours before midnight on New Year's.

In some countries they burn everything
when the year ends, to make a space for the new.
This has to do with the darkness
that keeps coming earlier through December,
and that imperceptible, frightening change
when it stops diminishing your days.
You get used to the encroachment of night—
it seems like a cheat that it turns
just when you start to give in to it. You've had
to give up so much just to get this far.
Then you may get drunk with it
and start giving away things you really need.

Your family, your possessions, all want you
to care for them. It seems everything
is asking too much; there are still
cold months ahead, and no one is taking this
seriously. People who try to advise you
are worried themselves; they've noticed bridges
are higher than they thought, and more beautiful.
It all has to do with the first big snowfall
when everything stops and the large drifts cover
the dirty and broken things, and everyone stays
in bed all morning, and lets it fall.

THE YEAR OF THE HORSE

In the bank, paper lanterns
at twelve feet, festooned
across Romanesque arches, lower
the room's apparent height.
Above, the ceiling vaults skyward.
In the year 4676, the bank bends
to the neighborhood, as if its
cathedral gloom were the only
truly venerable tradition,
this holiday a makeshift
children's game of paper
lanterns and cardboard
cut-out characters. And horses!
Horses everywhere—
horses with Chinese eyes, their coats
sleek and brown, their long profiles.
The lanterns swing
gently as the doors close and open.

The cashier sorts dollar bills
near closing, and turns them
so the faces look up at her.
High up, beyond the lanterns,
by the back wall, a man
with a red carnation leans
over the railing and counts us
as we come in lines, as we drift
away, past the guard with the keys.
At three o'clock he turns the calendar
ahead. Grilles are pulled tight
across the marble entrance, displacing
a settled flock of drunks
who grumble from steps to sidewalk
and lie down at ease again
in the cold, calling heaven to witness.

Twilight at three o'clock,
the lamps come on, arching
long necks above the street, looking
down; they are pressing me down;
reflections swim on the pavement.
Old women with crooked backs
move ahead by cutting
back and forth; their eyes
are hard, deep in their faces
under black arched brows.
They hold coin purses
between both hands before them
tight as I imagine they might grab
the reins of a skittish team.
The lady with the tambourine
is going to run away with Jesus,
find her home in the sky, no more pain.

It is the year of the horse,
but the horses are not running.
The horses are standing still
and no one is riding them.
I see from their eyes
they are tame horses,
waiting all this time,
thousand-year blood in their veins,
bred to the one rider. A cold wind cuts
the corner, teasing the posters;
the horses on them quiver, ready to go.

A boy on a skateboard
zips through the intersection;
radio to his ear, he doesn't hear
the car horns, curses, he doesn't
care, but steers with his feet, quick

sure and he's gone. Like that
I'd ride away, without faith
or money. Bring me a horse
with slanted eyes, buy me a ticket
to that Christian heaven.

HEAT LIGHTNING

It was then the sky,
closed up for the night and silent,
started to give back the fires
of charged dust and water beads. Clouds
flashed and swelled without sound,
and sudden, quicksilver rivers split
the picture, shot down the sky,
broke up in streams and suddenly
disappeared! The impulse leapt,
charge to charge, for miles
like a thrown rocket whose light
blossomed, grew, and grew so large
until it burst into dark again.

And the yard was dark,
the walls were dark, and your face
faint, the color of glass.
The light in the sky went up
out of reach—whips, snakes
crackling out of their skins.
Giving it back, the sky
let go that tension of too much
light. This reckless disarming
declared itself free of the world
and of the sun's beauty. It had
nothing to do with us—it did not
give, but only spent light.

The night was hot and private;
the cavern of the garden sank
out of shadow, and between us
the green breath of the leaves
darkened, gathering drops
of water from the air. A blue-
white razor slit the sky, so far
away it was no threat, neither
any promise. Your face disappeared.
I knew we might take anything
simply then. Odors rose up;
the leaves asked silently to be touched.

I won't marry this earth
I said, but I'd felt the serpent fire
sting the vague clouds to life,
a form so sudden, accidentally
revealed—no, created—and I thought
I might change my mind, maybe let go
one skin, think it over.

PATRICK

Tonight the night watch is drunk in the garden,
muttering revolutionary ideas he is too sick
and sad to ever remember.
He tells his life story, which is all bad luck,
out loud in argument; he wants
revenge, not sympathy. I hope for sleep
but will not find it yet tonight.
The ceiling fan rattles and sighs in the half-
dark, moving heat across heat.
There is always something burning now,
the dry months, harmattan's choking dust
in the throat, a smell of smoke, the brush
scorched to drive out snakes and rodents,
clubbed to the ground for meat.
Palms and grasses turn to black ash
driven at the screens, powdered
death drifts over our skin, smell of fur
and sinews roasting. The night watch
has been drinking since noon
yesterday, for his brother who died.
He wants us to give him money
to send the body home; he wants to buy a stone
to carve his name deep; he wants to take out
an obituary in the *Daily Sketch*.
He has taken all the money we gave him
and stayed drunk two days, and he is angry
with himself, and with us, and wants more.

In the black heat I can feel
insects crawling across my skin—again
and again I turn to the light and see my body
stung with sweat and grit, red lines
of flushed capillaries, nothing moving.
Insubstantial bodies of mosquitoes hover
beyond the screen, and huge
uncanny moths with singed wings
beat at the garden lights. Now the lights
fade out; the sound of fans winds down
and as the power fails, night opens
and closes like the mouth of a great fish.

The night is for the dead, they say here.
A black weight covers my eyes, tamping my ears, hot,
silent and without any form.
My consciousness goes out from me in space
so far away I touch nothing—nothing
reaches me; all I hear
is the blood that thumps and floods my ears.
Then, very near, begins another sound—human
and beaten. Out of black nothing a forced
breathing, something utterly
far from speech—a voice cut loose in its own
loneness. The night watch is crying
in the garden, uttering long, childish sobs.
He has kicked over a bench
and stumbled over it; he is feeling his way
along the gate and walls; he is turning on
light switches, flipping them over and over—one
lamp to the next without effect, as if he could not
realize.

THE FAULT

"What shall I cry? All flesh is grass,
and all its beauty like the flower of
the field."

Isaiah, 40:6

Because the bread is sweet, but we eat it and we die,
so the fault is not ours, but is in us. Given life,
bones frail as grass, we run all green and burning
on the earth. Grass earth, grass branches, grass
fires burning in the cellar's heart. The grass is sweet;
the bread is burning in my heart. And all around the heart
is water; rich salt currents answer every beat in waves.

Bread goes living into the fire; its held breath grows
and grows. So mild, this swelling life, this sacrifice, the
grass, the flower, and the ripe grain dropping. Let me
only say we do not die for bread, we do not die as grass,
and our hunger for this life may never die at all. There are
some things I believe and for these I will feed you and you will
die, but not because the life was wrong. Do not believe

that life is wrong, though it is wrong for us, though we can't hold it.
On the sea's bottom the grass grows long; rising currents
sway it back and forth—we can't breathe there, but in that
slow light lobsters are grazing, loathe to interruption.
We can't breathe there; it is not ours, but it is good, it is
burning even there, so sweet and the sea's deep flowers are all
brilliant. We know then we are water that must live in air

and burn, but how can we know this, how can we know even
what to cry, if we should cry for the flower or the seed,
or the full grain dropping? I know if there is a fault
it is in us like the fire in wood unnoticed until in a dry time
its hunger for air leaps out. There is a fault in the earth
where it opens, where grass pushes up, slowly pressing to find
a way. You must understand the fault is in us where we break—

but how can we break if we are grass, how can we burn if we are
water, how can we die when life is given us? Only what is given
is not ours; it is good and we would take it—our hunger
does not want to finish or destroy, but by taking our lives
whole, by taking life not ours as it is in us, we over-reach
ourselves and living longs for more, to leap out of this life,
this time, this self, this gift, this hesitating sacrifice.

LAGOS: TARGET PRACTICE

for John Humphreys

From the balcony, high above Five Cowrie Creek,
the islands of the city move out
in the dark, stepping silently down to the ocean.
We are shooting into the garden, steadying
our aim on the backs of chairs. Where generators
turn all night, in the walled compounds
spotted with little lights, broken glass
glints along the walls in points
and night guards stroke their torches
among the shrubbery and flowers. Bright
high-rises, lit from within, flame tall
like gas lamps burning from the center,
and the day's wash moves in the night air,
weak angels clinging at every window.
I aim across the water, choose one
window, and fire—the light does not move;
the pellet bounces on the gravel below.

The expressway is dead black, shot through
by twin lights—meteors
across the fly-over, dipping into the unlit
boroughs, along the lost path, past check points
where police wait by smoky fires
behind barricades of fenders, oil drums,
lost mufflers and cement blocks; no warning
until you catch them in your beams and brake and skid.
Someone is searching in the semi-dark
of his car's interior for important papers.
Flashlights shine in the deep corners;
tire jack, wrench, gas can, machete . . . Police
jab at the air with clubs. Their rifles
bang softly against their soft, moving bodies.

Close one eye and fire for the man
they didn't let go. Ping on the metal shade
of the garden lamp; a near miss.
Beyond them are miles of dense hot streets
with no lights at all. These sectors

are invisible from the balcony tonight, black holes
in the night-scape, unrecorded by instruments.
Mud houses, green glow of sewers, the strip
of soiled cloth over the door, and men with machetes,
knives and guns moving out on their errands.

On your left cheek a smear of blood hardens.
Our only kill, the gorged mosquito split
her sides at a blow. The fever she carries
is doused in quinine, kept low in the blood
but there, always waiting
and though we are protected, we are not safe.
Smoke rises, smell of kerosene and rubber smouldering.
It is long past midnight. In the yard below
a guard walks a shepherd pup on rounds,
training him to heel. He carefully
ignores the ripped leaves and pellets on stone
rebounding. Bad shots. Always the guards run away.
Boats go down the creek silently, without lights.
It could be the robbers coming at last.
It could be someone running from the police,
floated past the city into the harbor face down,
someone they have already named dead,
one of the failed soldiers, or nobody . . .

We do not fire at the boats. We are waiting.
We are waiting for the robbers or the police;
we are waiting for the next insurrection.
We are drinking brandy and shooting in the dark,
and though we are drunk by now, and our gun is a toy,
we feel ready, we think we will know what to do.

RECOVERY

Fever 100° is rational, newly
bright and inspired.
In this disorder, damp air
settling in the sheets like a new
malaise, the bed crumbled, hot,
among all the week's bottles
and spoons, I am myself again, empty,
looking out.

The wine-muddled gardener rants at the window
—stories begun in the middle, some quarrel
or plan gone too far, old gossip
and I feel—brief panic of sense!—how
I must reenter and take my life
out of weakness, in fever and in all desire,
must take this messy chaos of the
mind, and make it all
visible! I can name task on task,
domestic and spiritual, that needs to begin.
But effort is out of reach; still
the bath, breakfast, tidying the room,
and sounds of the world outside blooming
and fretting the morning, exhaust.

I have spent years chasing order
one action at a time, and still
it falls apart when I lie down!
I open my eyes and say: years gone nowhere.
And I have been busy, choosing the lesser part,
chasing off visions like dust.
Locked in the time-step of grown-up, polite,
still looking forward, I tripped.
Now look up, worry myself
with spots on the ceiling. Get busy, busy!

How to reenter from weakness, how can I
make my life visible when the fever
leaving me is more brilliant than I am,

when the whole astonishing world is no
taskmaster, but is, clearly,
itself and no more—when from weakness spirit wakens
muttering in the garden?

TALKING TO MYSELF

The mouths of my body are asking for you.
They whisper and wait for answers; they make little
sucking noises and open wide, wanting to be fed.
Remembering the taste of you, they can't understand
why you don't come around anymore.
Rosebud mouths of my nipples, twin virgins
press themselves forward to be kissed good-night;
mouths of my belly, mouths in the palm of my hand
keep repeating to me how your body is shaped.
Mouth of the delicate neck flesh, base of my throat
that kissed your fingers, that tasted your breath
when you pressed your face down to that shelter.
Whale mouth of my arms, opening
to swallow you, and closing still hungry, teeth-
fingers, nails that nibbled your back, bit down
when you struggled in my arms, hooked you and held on.
Ocean mouth where you came into me,
womb full of swimming mouths, seawater, mewing
of hungry birds who dive for the fish the waves toss.
This world of creation, no longer provided for.
I know about endings, don't like to complain,
but I have so many hungry mouths in me, mouths
that you are the father of, mouths that do not understand
abandonment. They whimper and howl all night,
and only subside, little cannibals, when they feed
on one another. Thigh touches thigh, and tongue quiets
the wrist and the palm of the hand, while the other
hand goes searching below, offering
a finger to suck on, salt flesh, and nothing to drink.

FIRE

From the hollows under rocks, from the hidden
seed in the ground, from grasses that kept,
secretly, their small fire near the roots,
this rain is taking everything away. Boats,
fences, the undersides of shingles, feel
the rain slide through the cracks, finding
and taking the hoarded warmth. And not only
wood and earth, but bodies chill, giving up
the memory of their last embraces, like leaves
caught in the fork of a tree, held by the wish
to be covered. Rain pulls the leaves down
and lifts the footprints under windows.
It rains until the gutters fill and start to break
away from eaves, until the low ground
floods and animals are scared from their dens.
When you wake and hear a rain like this—
give up. Confess where you have hidden your desires.
Let the rain take the fire away.

IV

NOT THE ATLANTIC

This poem is not about the Atlantic, but it is nearby,
so close it can hear the boats offshore, and the waves

falling over, the white-bellied terns crying over their nests.
So close we can see it whenever we want to, which is not often,

and never for long, because if anything is interesting,
it's not the Atlantic. Flat, and too wide to measure,

with a color that really belongs to the sky, there's nothing
there to make the mind hold still. And when the poem learns

the truth about waves, how they travel light, like rumors,
and nothing goes with them, the poem is ready to give up!

It says the Atlantic is too cold to go into right now
and it stays there at the edge with whatever it finds there: wooden

pulleys and bottles, a dogfish dead in the sand, smooth stones,
and beach grass bent over in wind. An injured gull

picks seaweed for insects, and below this hill the Atlantic
left years ago, a girl urges a white horse across the rim of

exploding breakers, their blonde manes all waving and running behind.
But still, none of this is about the Atlantic,

because the Atlantic is impossible; because it is about things
being here, but not about the things themselves. And we're here

at the edge, where things we can name are discarded, and sand
bars trip waves to collapse at our feet. On this shore

which is not the Atlantic, with these nearby birds who are not
the Atlantic, as sand is not, or water, or any other words.

And if not the Atlantic, then none of these—grass, fire, hill,
and we are not here in this poem and no objects are near us.

HERRING COVE

Body of water—
a harbor seal is lost in you, offshore,
turning his head to look for playmates.

Mutter, mutter—the sun has gone down,
the moon rose early, lost
her transparency, white face very calm.

Tides aren't pulled to the land
but to the sky; they climb the beach
to get closer. In the sky

are many bodies drowning. Body of light,
body of water, climb up
the steps of sand where the sea comes, back

to the brightness of cars and their journeys,
incandescence of kitchens—go on
and let those two look for one another

all night. The moon can find him
in the water, and hold him, and the moon
will be out all night. Now boats

ride low in the water, and men hurry in,
tired of the sea and wanting the moon
to stop pulling them. The sky must be

so empty, because the moon seems to want
everything it touches tonight. A seal dives
and comes up alone, and water pulls

the sky around it, one color
when the moon keeps rising, and there is no
horizon and no one will be there again.

WE HAVE LIVED IN GREAT HOUSES

1

Boats that crossed between islands
at night found their way; the deep
curve of their hulls was ours,

and we have had
the grey wake behind us at morning
with no shore in sight

and wooden chairs damp under our hands.
We had the island, shaped
like a footprint, slept in beds

other hands prepared for us,
yet what was offered seemed more
than anyone could have intended.

Under our beds quick rivers sang
throughout the town, notes older
than any our tongues knew.

2

Once in midsummer, snow
fell through a night without darkness,
when the sun floated high among mountains,

stuck to that horizon
whose peaks were black fingers—
on that mountain where grass grew on rooftops

and earth underfoot was hard
with reflected light. Then the sun found us
sleeping, its light in our faces.

Then the snow was a white lid closing
over the hollows of valleys—rock walls
that drive the sky back from their wound.

Then our dreams
came to the surface to drink, and wrote
their changing names on our faces.

3

We dreamed that the house would remain
like a song learned deep in the mouth.
Pale boards struggle to hold up

the space where we are standing,
and a rock in a field says others
will be raising themselves from the ground

again, and there are stairs I will climb
one day, when the house is built.
We have lived in great houses; they kept us

through nights, and in full light of day
we owned them, as anyone might own
the space inside his body. They are gone

when we have climbed up in them, up long
staircases into rooms our desires made
beautiful. And the stairs are gone

when we turn, as the boat retreats,
loses sight of the shore; we appear
to be growing smaller then, and it is our

leaving which loses them. We climbed out,
stepped from the rocking hold
with our gypsy bags clutched; we stepped out

like stepping away from our bodies—a hand
reached for what was held
and our hands opened to give it.

THE ROCK

Water coming toward us now. The rock
moves more slowly; vegetable bodies stroke
my legs as I swim past, and the bay fills
with boats. Water is generous, lifting them
to the level of houses, pushing
up from beneath, pushing our bodies away
from the bottom, heads out of the water.

The girl on the beach has taken off her shirt
to allow the dark-skinned man beside her
to stroke her breasts. I swim farther out.
I can't hear you now. If I stay here
it will always be this beginning,

salt water pressing between my legs,
so warm the parts of my body lose distinction.
I see my breasts floating, lifted
by water, the current a soft tongue circling. I can't
hear you now. I swim as if I am not moving.
I am bringing the rock closer; the rock
touches the bottom and water is covering it—
I will hold on to the rock underwater.

THE SEASON

Cranberries, apples, no walnuts,
mussels and clams and rosehips, bay
laurel and wintergreen sharp
in your mouth. Salt hay on the
garden, kale through December—
the dug earth breathes
through its fingers,
roots clenched around stones. Deer
keep the same trails; we follow;
we drag the big buck through the snow,
but the rabbit is light in our hands,
his head hanging down. Fish go into
deep water now; the blonde mane
of the dunes tangles in wind
and the owl turns around in mid-air
to stare back at us. The red fox
who stole the terns' children
in August gets hungry again
but stays low, hearing voices.
Everyone gets hungry again, and will get
hungrier. Lucky we know what to do.
Blood ovals melt into snow;
something sniffs after, and entrails,
flung on the ground, steaming,
disappear, and someone has eaten them.
Pine cones are shaken for nuts, bear-
berries tasted and stored; small insects
feel the rocks above them turned over.
Gulls beat clams against rocks
and pull the bodies in shreds. The wind
warns us—false prophet or not—
it warns us: winter will strip
the woods to bone; in that sharp
light, held back since spring,
our shadows will stretch
long, among the starved trees.

WINGS

The marsh hawk flies low, hunting
nests in the grass. I strip
plum branches hurriedly, charged
as if that wing's shadow touched me,

spread like a fierce, transforming angel
on the ground. Nobody wants to be saved!
Hurry, the storm is coming;
thunder is hungry for anything free.

My house has thin boards and it tries to fly
away when the wind comes to lift it.
Wasps sing in religious
fury over the door. Golden, bit by

sun-fire, all day they have been stinging
the ripe plums.
Now they fold their wings
in the tight corners under eaves.

Their hard jaws
make wood houses paper; purple nectar
falls slowly, in heavy drops like wine.
Paper houses, sustenance of fruit,

the purple welts swelling
under my skin, venomous kisses
as I fall through the guarded
entrance into the other life.

FROM EXILE

1

The boats go by in another world.
I am living on shore with one sparrow.
He sings the whole morning outside my door,
but when I am quiet, late mornings in bed,
or sitting at my desk unmoving,
he comes nearer, bangs on the stove-pipe,
waking an echo to ask if I've gone.

He struts on the roof, flat-footed,
eats bugs from the stair-rail, preens.
Then my monster shadow
at the door stands up
to make his wings beat fast.

No one speaks to me here.
Night-walkers, spirits with legs,
leave illegible prints in the sand. Unheard,
never-seen strangers—the rumored fox,
snake, skunk, rabbit—give nothing away.
A light from the step won't freeze them;
they're gone when a foot hits the floor.

Alone here, I scare like a bird,
quick as the thought of fear. My own
shadow in the window makes my breath come fast.
When stars move past me, I want to fly out
into the wider dark.

2

Every day the same: before me
the ocean, saying *wish, wish, wish,*
all night and all day, overhead
warnings of seabirds, white against the sky,
dangling live, struggling fish in their beaks
given in token of love, or bargains
to be sealed. Behind me, the busy town
in whose crowds I was often lost,
language of buying and selling salt,

an island light, oiled with sun,
the peoples' faces brown,
and in their palms, folded, hidden maps
on which our home does not appear.
I'm barely real to them, have gone unnoticed
carrying secret bulletins in my clothes,
professions of love that could bring down governments,
letters with no address or postage, still sent out
whenever they are too many to hold.

Always sand and rocks, always stars at night.
Boats fly low in the window—small lights, deep voices.
They carry messages, cargo and guns,
and huge weird fish reeking with news of the depths,
and black silent oil in steel tanks,
giving yet no hint of fire. Sail-boats, whiter than
gulls, go out for the day, and the ferry crossing,
the curious faces. The boats are listening to the shore,
feeling the bottom with sensitive instruments.
Each night a beacon strokes the shore and returns.
I stand on the hill to let it touch me—
white light, white skin, as if I could finally dare
to be seen. The blind beam revolves,
light to its own purpose. I am safe; I am blessed.

3

The boats are no closer than stars;
sometimes the horizon pulls them over.
Their hulls divide
the water by touch—blind undersides.

They used to be many.
They used to be white cities, measuring
the distance between islands.

Now planes fly overhead
carrying death somewhere else.

I should have gone back long ago.
I'm afraid all the others have returned
without me, and my voice is forgotten.
I'm afraid that the stars that moved past me
were not the true stars, but jets
or meteors destined to earth.

If I do not return there will be no one
left to speak my name. I've raised three
bright shirts on the line to call for rescue.
There's little time.

You, if this reaches you,
don't let them place my name among the dead.
Say I am coming back. Show them my letters.

CYNTHIA HUNTINGTON

Born in Meadville, Pennsylvania, in 1951,
Cynthia Huntington is a graduate of Michigan
State University and Middlebury College. She
has been a fellow at the Fine Arts Work Center
in Provincetown, where she lived for several
years. Her poems have appeared in numerous
magazines and in 1984 she was awarded a fellow-
ship grant in poetry from the National Endow-
ment for the Arts.

Production Notes

This book was designed by Roger Eggers. Composition and paging were done on the Quadex Composing System and typesetting on the Compugraphic 8400 by the design and production staff of University of Hawaii Press.

The text and display typeface is Compugraphic Bembo.

Offset presswork and binding were done by Malloy Lithographing, Inc. Text paper is Glatfelter Offset Vellum, basis 50.